HOLLY CARLISLE

Leading the Way or Managing the Course

A Comparative Study of Leadership and Management

This book was professionally typeset on Reedsy.
Find out more at reedsy.com

Contents

I

Part One

1

Chapter 1: Defining Leadership

Leadership is a dynamic process of influencing individuals or groups towards the achievement of a shared goal. It goes beyond authority and encompasses the ability to inspire, guide, and mobilize others to contribute their best efforts. At its core, leadership is about navigating challenges, fostering collaboration, and driving positive change within an organization.

Fundamental Elements of Leadership:

- **Vision:** Effective leaders articulate a compelling vision that inspires and aligns team members toward a common objective. This clarity of purpose serves as a guiding force, motivating individuals to work collectively and with purpose.

The Essence of Vision - Case Study: A compelling instance of visionary leadership can be observed in the journey of Tim Cook, the CEO of Apple Inc., and the late Steve Jobs, Apple's co-founder. In the early 2000s, Apple faced challenges and needed a new direction. Jobs, with his unparalleled vision, envisioned a future where technology seamlessly integrates into daily life through aesthetically pleasing and user-friendly devices.

The articulation of this vision led to the development of groundbreaking products such as the iPod, iPhone, and iPad. Jobs' vision extended beyond the mere creation of gadgets; it aimed to redefine how individuals interact with technology. The result was a transformative shift in the tech industry, setting Apple apart as an innovator and trendsetter.

Under Jobs' leadership, Apple's visionary approach not only revitalized the company but also influenced the entire tech landscape. The shared vision of creating revolutionary products fueled a culture of innovation within Apple, attracting top talent and fostering a commitment to excellence.

Even after Jobs' passing, Tim Cook, as the successor, continued to uphold and evolve Apple's visionary legacy. Cook's leadership maintained a focus on innovation, sustainability, and social responsibility, demonstrating the enduring impact of a shared vision on organizational culture and success.

The Apple case study illustrates how a clear and inspiring vision, when effectively communicated and pursued, can drive innovation, reshape industries, and create a lasting legacy. It serves as a testament to the enduring power of visionary leadership in navigating challenges, inspiring teams, and achieving remarkable success.

- **Inspiration:** Leaders inspire through their actions, words, and demeanor. They create a positive and motivating environment, fostering a sense of enthusiasm and commitment among team members. By embodying the values they advocate, leaders encourage others to strive for excellence.

The Role of Inspiration - Case Study: A striking example of leadership through inspiration is observed in the leadership style of Nelson Mandela, the revered anti-apartheid revolutionary and former President of South Africa. Mandela's life and leadership journey epitomize the transformative impact of inspiration on individuals and societies.

During his 27-year imprisonment, Mandela became a symbol of resilience and unwavering commitment to justice. Upon his release in 1990, instead of harboring resentment, Mandela embraced reconciliation and forgiveness, setting a powerful example for a fractured nation emerging from decades of racial strife.

Mandela's ability to inspire went beyond words; it was deeply rooted in his actions and demeanor. His commitment to inclusivity, equality, and unity inspired not only his fellow activists but also captivated the global community. The vision he articulated—of a "rainbow nation" built on the principles of democracy and equality—became a beacon of hope for South Africa and the world.

Under Mandela's leadership, South Africa underwent a peaceful transition to majority rule, dismantling the institutionalized system of apartheid. His inspirational leadership style was marked by humility, empathy, and an unyielding belief in the human spirit's capacity for change.

The case of Nelson Mandela showcases the profound impact that an inspirational leader can have on individuals and society at large. Mandela's ability to inspire transcended political boundaries, leaving an indelible mark on history. This case study serves as a poignant reminder of how inspiration, when embodied by a leader, can catalyze positive change, unite diverse communities, and foster a shared commitment to a better future.

- **Influence:** Leadership involves the ability to influence people and decisions. Leaders leverage their credibility, communication skills, and expertise to shape perspectives, build consensus, and drive organizational initiatives forward.

The Role of Influence – A Case Study: A compelling illustration of leadership through influence is evident in the career of Angela Merkel, the former Chancellor of Germany. Merkel's leadership style, characterized by astute decision-making and diplomatic finesse, exemplifies the transformative power of influence on the global stage.

During her tenure, Merkel faced formidable challenges, including the Eurozone crisis and the Syrian refugee influx. Her approach to these complex issues showcased her ability to wield influence effectively. Merkel's leadership was marked by a commitment to consensus-building and negotiation, transcending traditional partisan divides.

One notable example of Merkel's influential leadership was during the Eurozone crisis. Through a combination of strategic communication, economic expertise, and diplomatic efforts, she played a key role in orchestrating European responses to stabilize the financial markets and prevent the collapse of the euro.

Furthermore, Merkel's influence was pivotal in navigating the humanitarian challenges posed by the Syrian refugee crisis. By advocating for a collective European response and demonstrating compassion, Merkel not only shaped the discourse but also influenced other European leaders to adopt a more empathetic and cooperative stance.

Merkel's leadership legacy underscores how influence, when wielded with strategic acumen and a commitment to common goals, can shape policies, foster collaboration, and address complex challenges. This case study serves as a valuable example for leaders seeking to understand how effective influence can be harnessed to drive positive change on both national and international scales.

- **Adaptability:** Successful leaders demonstrate adaptability in the face of change. They navigate uncertainty with resilience, make informed decisions, and guide their teams through evolving landscapes, fostering a culture of agility and innovation.

The Importance of Adaptability – A Case Study: An illuminating example of leadership adaptability is found in the tenure of Satya Nadella, the CEO of Microsoft. Nadella's leadership journey is marked by his adeptness at steering Microsoft through a transformative period in the tech industry, showcasing the critical role of adaptability in leadership.

Upon assuming the role of CEO in 2014, Nadella inherited a technology landscape undergoing rapid change. Traditional software models were giving way to cloud computing, mobile devices were becoming ubiquitous, and Microsoft faced challenges in remaining competitive. In response, Nadella undertook a strategic shift, steering the company towards a cloud-first, mobile-first approach.

Nadella's adaptability was evident in his willingness to reshape Microsoft's organizational culture. He emphasized collaboration, openness to new ideas, and a focus on innovation.

Under his leadership, Microsoft embraced cloud technologies with platforms like Azure and adopted a more agile development approach, allowing the company to stay relevant in a rapidly evolving tech landscape.

The importance of Nadella's adaptability became even more apparent during the COVID-19 pandemic. Microsoft, under his guidance, quickly pivoted to remote work, accelerating digital transformation initiatives, and addressing new challenges posed by the global crisis.

The case of Satya Nadella underscores how adaptability in leadership is not just about responding to change but proactively shaping an organization's trajectory in a dynamic environment. His ability to navigate technological shifts, reshape corporate culture, and lead during a global crisis demonstrates the indispensable nature of adaptability in effective leadership. This example serves as a valuable lesson for leaders aspiring to thrive in an ever-changing business landscape.

- **Accountability:** Leaders hold themselves and others accountable for results. This involves taking responsibility for actions, admitting mistakes, and ensuring that individuals within the team are empowered and supported in their roles.

The Necessity for Accountability - A Case Study: A compelling example of the necessity for accountability in leadership is observed in the Tylenol crisis of 1982 and the subsequent actions of James E. Burke, then CEO of Johnson & Johnson. The crisis began when seven people in the Chicago area died after ingesting Extra-Strength Tylenol capsules that had been tampered with, resulting in cyanide poisoning.

Faced with a life-threatening situation and a potential threat to public trust, Burke took immediate and decisive action. Johnson & Johnson, under Burke's leadership, initiated a nationwide recall of 31 million bottles of Tylenol, costing the company millions of dollars. Burke demonstrated accountability by prioritizing public safety over short-term financial concerns.

In response to the crisis, Burke also co-operated fully with law enforcement and the Food and Drug Administration (FDA), actively participating in the investigations. He communicated transparently with the public, providing updates and guidance on the situation. Burke's accountability extended beyond the crisis management phase; he led efforts to introduce tamper-evident packaging to prevent similar incidents in the future.

James E. Burke's handling of the Tylenol crisis exemplifies the critical importance of accountability in leadership. By taking responsibility for the situation, making difficult decisions in the interest of public safety, and implementing long-term preventive measures, Burke not only safeguarded the reputation of Johnson & Johnson but also set a high standard for corporate accountability in the face of adversity. This case study serves as a poignant reminder of how accountability, when demonstrated by leaders, is not only essential for organizational integrity but also plays a crucial role in maintaining public trust..

In summarizing the exploration of leadership fundamentals, we extract key traits that define effective leadership. Visionary insight shapes a clear path forward, while inspirational influence ignites enthusiasm among team members. Strategic influence allows leaders to navigate complexities, and adaptive agility ensures resilience in the face of uncertainty. Proactive accountability remains paramount, as leaders take responsibility, prioritize integrity, and confront challenges transparently. Together, these traits form the essence of effective leadership, providing a robust foundation for navigating the intricacies of leadership with confidence and purpose.

2

Chapter 2: Defining Management

Management is the dynamic process of coordinating and organizing resources within an organization to achieve predefined goals. It involves strategic planning to set objectives, organizing resources efficiently, and controlling activities through monitoring and adjustments. The cyclical nature of management emphasizes its adaptability to the evolving needs of the organization. Successful management demands effective leadership, strong communication skills, and a nuanced understanding of organizational dynamics to foster a collaborative and productive working environment.

1. **Planning:** Planning is a vital aspect of management, providing a strategic framework for achieving organizational goals. It clarifies objectives, minimizes uncertainties, and aligns efforts toward a common purpose. By anticipating challenges and optimizing resources, planning enables organizations to adapt to changes, stay competitive, and sustain long-term success. In essence, it serves as the foundation for effective management, empowering orga-

nizations to proactively shape their future and capitalize on opportunities.

Significance of Planning - A Case Study: A compelling example highlighting the significance of planning is evident in Toyota's renowned Production System. In the 1950s, Toyota faced economic challenges and limited resources in post-war Japan. To overcome these obstacles, the company implemented a meticulous planning system that would revolutionize the automotive industry.

Toyota's planning strategy involved just-in-time manufacturing, which aimed to minimize inventory and production costs. By carefully synchronizing production with customer demand, Toyota could reduce waste, optimize resources, and enhance overall efficiency. This planning approach not only allowed Toyota to navigate resource constraints but also led to shorter production lead times and improved product quality.

During the 1970s oil crisis, the significance of Toyota's planning became even more apparent. While other automakers struggled with excess inventory of fuel-inefficient vehicles, Toyota's just-in-time system allowed them to swiftly adjust production to meet the demand for smaller, more fuel-efficient cars. This adaptability, stemming from meticulous planning, positioned Toyota ahead of its competitors and solidified its reputation for efficiency and innovation.

The case of Toyota's Production System underscores how strategic planning can be a transformative force, enabling organizations to navigate challenges, optimize resources, and respond effectively to changing circumstances. It remains a benchmark example of the enduring impact of thorough planning on organizational success.

1. **Organizing:** Organizing, in the context of management, refers to the systematic arrangement and structuring of resources within an organization to facilitate the effective pursuit of predetermined goals. This process involves creating a framework of roles, responsibilities, and relationships to ensure optimal coordination and collaboration among individuals and departments. Organizing is essential for establishing order, promoting efficiency, and enabling seamless communication and workflow. It encompasses the design of organizational structures, the allocation of tasks, and the establishment of reporting hierarchies to streamline operations and enhance overall productivity.

A Picture of Organization - A Case Study: An illustrative example of effective organizing in management is evident in the operations of Amazon's fulfillment centers. These centers play a crucial role in the company's global supply chain and exemplify meticulous organizational planning.

Amazon's fulfillment centers are strategically located to facilitate quick and cost-effective delivery. The organizational structure within these centers is finely tuned for efficiency, with clearly defined roles for various teams. Tasks are organized based on a systematic workflow, from receiving and storing inventory to picking, packing, and shipping orders.

The layout of the fulfillment centers is designed to minimize the time and effort required to process orders. Products are strategically placed, and the use of advanced technologies, such as robots and automation, enhances the overall efficiency of the operation.

The organizational design extends to the workforce, where

employees are trained for specific tasks, contributing to a streamlined and productive operation. Additionally, the use of technology for order tracking, inventory management, and quality control ensures a well-organized and coordinated process.

In essence, the success of Amazon's fulfillment centers is not only due to the vast scale of operations but also the result of effective organizing in management. The meticulous planning and structured organization within these centers contribute to Amazon's ability to fulfill a vast number of orders accurately and rapidly, showcasing the importance of organization in large-scale logistical operations.

Controlling: Controlling, in the context of management, refers to the process of monitoring, evaluating, and regulating activities within an organization to ensure they align with the established plans and objectives. It involves the systematic measurement of performance against predetermined standards and the implementation of corrective actions when necessary. The controlling function aims to identify deviations from the planned course, understand their causes, and take corrective measures to maintain or improve organizational performance. Through feedback mechanisms and continuous assessment, controlling enables managers to make informed decisions, enhance efficiency, and ensure the organization's overall success.

Controlling - A Case Study: Consider a manufacturing company committed to delivering high-quality products to its customers. In this context, controlling is exemplified through a robust quality control process.

The organization establishes specific quality standards and criteria for its products during the planning phase. As the production process unfolds, the quality control team systematically monitors the output, conducting inspections and tests to ensure that the products meet the predetermined quality benchmarks.

If deviations from the quality standards are identified—such as defects, variations, or inconsistencies—the controlling function comes into play. The management takes corrective actions, which may include halting production, adjusting manufacturing processes, or providing additional training to workers.

The feedback loop in quality control is crucial. It not only helps in identifying and rectifying issues promptly but also contributes to continuous improvement. Insights from quality control assessments can be used to refine production processes, enhance product design, and ultimately elevate the overall quality of the company's offerings.

In this way, controlling, as applied to quality control in manufacturing, is instrumental in ensuring that the organization delivers products that meet or exceed customer expectations while continually striving for operational excellence.

Effective management is characterized by a synthesis of key traits. Planning, a foundational trait, involves setting clear objectives and outlining tasks for efficient resource allocation. Organizing encompasses the systematic arrangement of roles and responsibilities, fostering collaboration and efficiency. Controlling is crucial for monitoring and regulating activities to align with established plans, ensuring a proactive approach to maintaining or enhancing organizational performance. Together, these traits form the bedrock of effective management, providing a robust framework for leaders to guide their teams, optimize resources, and navigate the dynamic landscape of organizational success.

3

Chapter 3: The Interplay Between Leadership and Management

The delicate balance between leadership and management is a linchpin for organizational success. While leadership sets the visionary direction, inspires teams, and catalyzes change, management provides the necessary structure, coordination, and control to translate those visions into tangible results. An organization thrives when this equilibrium is maintained – leaders guide the way, fostering innovation and motivation, while managers ensure the efficient execution of plans, resource optimization, and operational stability. The synergy between leadership and management is akin to a well-choreographed dance, where the strengths of both are harnessed to navigate complexities, adapt to change, and achieve sustainable growth. Striking this balance cultivates a dynamic, resilient, and forward-thinking organizational culture, where the pursuit of a shared vision harmonizes with the systematic orchestration of resources and tasks. Ultimately, it is the harmonious interplay of leadership and management that propels organizations toward their goals in an ever-evolving business landscape.

1. **Situational examples:**

A. Strategic Decision-Making:

Leadership: Leaders often play a pivotal role in strategic decision-making, envisioning the future direction of the organization and setting overarching goals. Their ability to articulate a compelling vision influences the strategic course of the company.

Management: Managers are integral to the execution of strategic decisions. They translate the vision into actionable plans, allocate resources, and coordinate the efforts of teams to ensure the strategic objectives are met. The effective implementation of strategies requires managerial expertise.

B. Team Motivation and Development:

Leadership: Leaders inspire and motivate teams by fostering a shared sense of purpose and vision. They empower individuals, encourage creativity, and promote a positive and collaborative work environment.

Management: Managers, while overseeing day-to-day operations, play a crucial role in motivating and developing their teams. They provide guidance, set performance expectations, and offer opportunities for skill development. A motivated and skilled team is essential for achieving organizational goals.

C. Change Management:

Leadership: Leaders are at the forefront of driving organizational change. They articulate the need for change, communicate the vision for the future, and inspire individuals to embrace new ways of working.

Management: Managers are responsible for implementing and managing change at the operational level. They ensure that teams understand and adapt to new processes, provide the necessary resources, and monitor progress. The success of change initiatives relies on effective leadership and management collaboration.

- **Real Life Examples of Leaders and Managers Who Perfected the Interplay of Leadership and Management:**

Indra Nooyi (Former CEO of PepsiCo):
Indra Nooyi is recognized for her adept integration of leadership and management during her tenure as the CEO of PepsiCo. As a leader, she emphasized the importance of purpose-driven leadership and spearheaded the company's commitment to sustainability and healthier product offerings. Nooyi's leadership style involved setting a compelling vision for the company's future. Simultaneously, as a manager, she implemented strategic initiatives, managed the diversification of PepsiCo's product portfolio, and focused on operational efficiency. Nooyi's success is attributed to her ability to unite visionary leadership with effective management practices.

Mary Barra (Chair and CEO of General Motors):
Mary Barra is recognized for her adept management and leadership at General Motors. As a leader, she has steered the company through significant transformations, emphasizing innovation and sustainability. Barra's leadership involves setting a clear vision for GM's future, including a commitment to electric and autonomous vehicles. On the management front, she has overseen the restructuring of the company, focused on

operational efficiency, and implemented strategic initiatives to keep GM competitive in the rapidly evolving automotive industry.

Sheryl Sandberg (Former COO of Facebook):

- Sheryl Sandberg, as the former Chief Operating Officer of Facebook, exemplifies the integration of leadership and management. As a leader, Sandberg is known for her advocacy of empowering women in the workplace and her focus on fostering a dynamic corporate culture. In terms of management, she played a key role in scaling Facebook's operations, overseeing business strategies, and driving the company's profitability. Sandberg's ability to combine visionary leadership with effective day-to-day management contributed to Facebook's growth during her tenure.

4

Chapter 4: Training for Leadership

1. Educational Pathways

Developing leadership skills is a continuous journey that can be pursued through various educational pathways. Here are several educational avenues to enhance and cultivate leadership skills:

Formal Education:

- Pursue a Bachelor's Degree: Many universities offer programs in business administration, management, or leadership studies. These degrees provide a solid foundation in leadership principles and management practices.
- Earn a Master's in Business Administration (MBA): An MBA program offers advanced coursework in leadership, strategic management, and organizational behavior. It is a comprehensive educational path for aspiring leaders.
- Leadership Development Programs:
- Corporate Training Programs: Many companies offer in-house leadership development programs to enhance the

skills of their employees. These programs often cover topics such as communication, decision-making, and team management.
- Leadership Certificates: Various institutions and professional organizations provide leadership certificate programs. These programs offer focused training on specific leadership competencies.

Online Courses and Webinars:

- Platforms like Coursera, LinkedIn Learning, and Udemy offer a plethora of online courses focused on leadership development. These courses cover topics ranging from emotional intelligence to strategic leadership.
- Executive Education Programs:
- Attend Workshops and Seminars: Leadership workshops and seminars conducted by industry experts provide valuable insights and practical strategies. These short-term programs are often tailored to specific leadership challenges.
- Executive Leadership Programs: Renowned institutions offer executive education programs designed for mid-to-senior-level professionals. These programs provide an in-depth exploration of leadership concepts.
- Professional Development Programs:
- Industry-Specific Training: Many industries have specialized leadership training programs that address the unique challenges and dynamics within that sector.
- Mentorship Programs: Engaging in mentorship relationships with experienced leaders provides practical, on-the-job learning opportunities.

- Networking and Conferences:
- Attend Leadership Conferences: Participation in leadership conferences allows individuals to learn from successful leaders, gain insights into industry trends, and expand their professional network.
- Join Professional Associations: Many professional associations offer leadership development resources, events, and networking opportunities.
- Continuous Learning and Reading:
- Read Leadership Literature: Books on leadership by renowned authors provide valuable perspectives and strategies. Works by authors like John C. Maxwell, Stephen R. Covey, and Simon Sinek are widely recognized.
- Subscribe to Journals and Publications: Academic journals and business publications often feature articles on leadership theories, case studies, and best practices.
- Soft Skills Training:
- Communication Courses: Effective leadership requires strong communication skills. Taking courses on public speaking, interpersonal communication, and negotiation can be beneficial.
- Emotional Intelligence Training: Courses focusing on emotional intelligence help leaders understand and manage emotions, both their own and those of others.

Combining formal education, practical experiences, and continuous learning through various avenues can create a well-rounded approach to leadership development. Tailoring these pathways to individual goals and preferences enhances the effectiveness of the leadership learning journey.

2. Experiential Pathways

Experiential pathways play a crucial role in developing leadership skills by providing hands-on, practical learning opportunities. These pathways focus on real-world experiences that allow individuals to apply and refine their leadership abilities. Here are several experiential avenues for developing leadership skills:

On-the-Job Experience:

- Project Leadership: Taking on leadership roles within projects allows individuals to practice decision-making, team coordination, and problem-solving in a real-world context.
- Cross-Functional Assignments: Rotations or assignments in different departments provide exposure to diverse challenges, fostering adaptability and a broader understanding of organizational dynamics.

Team Leadership:

- Team Projects: Leading a team on specific projects encourages collaboration, conflict resolution, and the ability to motivate and inspire team members toward common goals.
- Volunteer Leadership: Leading a volunteer or community organization provides a unique opportunity to develop leadership skills while making a positive impact on the community.

Leadership in Student Organizations:

- Student Government: Participating in student government or leadership roles in campus organizations hones leadership skills in a collaborative and dynamic environment.
- Club or Society Leadership: Leading a club or society fosters organizational and interpersonal skills, as individuals coordinate events, manage budgets, and engage with diverse group members.

Internships and Apprenticeships:

- Internship Leadership: Internship experiences allow individuals to work in a professional setting, taking on responsibilities that contribute to organizational goals and developing leadership skills.
- Apprenticeships: Learning directly from experienced leaders through apprenticeship programs provides a practical understanding of leadership in a specific industry.

Entrepreneurial Ventures:

- Start-Up Leadership: Founding or joining a start-up exposes individuals to the challenges of entrepreneurship, requiring them to take on multifaceted leadership roles and make strategic decisions.
- Business Ownership: Managing and leading a small business provides hands-on experience in decision-making, resource allocation, and team management.

Simulations and Role-Playing:

- Leadership Simulations: Virtual or in-person simulations allow individuals to practice leadership skills in controlled scenarios, facilitating the development of strategic thinking and decision-making abilities.
- Role-Playing Exercises: Role-playing scenarios help individuals enhance communication, conflict resolution, and negotiation skills in a safe and controlled environment

Professional Development Programs:

- Leadership Development Programs: Participating in structured leadership development programs offered by organizations, which may include mentorship, coaching, and skill-building workshops, provides targeted experiential learning.
- Action Learning Projects: Engaging in projects that directly address organizational challenges allows individuals to apply leadership principles to real-world problems.

Networking and Industry Involvement:

- Professional Associations: Active involvement in professional associations provides opportunities to engage with industry leaders, participate in committees, and lead initiatives, contributing to leadership development.
- Conferences and Seminars: Attending industry-specific events enables individuals to network, share insights, and stay updated on trends, fostering leadership growth.

Experiential pathways are dynamic and adaptive, allowing individuals to learn and grow by facing real challenges. Combining experiential learning with reflection and feedback enhances the effectiveness of these pathways, contributing to the holistic development of leadership skills.

3. Various Leadership Development Programs and Noted Graduates

General Electric's (GE) Leadership Development Program:

- **Overview:** General Electric is renowned for its Leadership Development Program (LDP), an initiative designed to cultivate and nurture future leaders within the company.
- **Approach:** The LDP at GE is a comprehensive program that involves rotational assignments, formal training, mentorship, and coaching. Participants are exposed to various functions of the company, promoting a holistic understanding of GE's operations.
- **Results:** Many top executives at GE, including former CEO Jeff Immelt, attribute their success to the LDP. The program has been instrumental in producing leaders with a broad skill set, strategic thinking, and the ability to drive innovation. Alumni of the program often hold key leadership positions within the organization.

Microsoft's Leadership Development Program:

- **Overview:** Microsoft, a technology giant, has implemented a Leadership Development Program that focuses on identifying and developing high-potential individuals.
- **Approach:** The program at Microsoft includes a combi-

nation of on-the-job experiences, mentoring by senior leaders, participation in cross-functional projects, and formal training sessions. It emphasizes the company's core leadership principles and values.

- **Results:** Microsoft's Leadership Development Program has been successful in producing leaders who contribute significantly to the company's growth and innovation. Alumni of the program have played key roles in the development and launch of major products, contributing to Microsoft's ongoing success in the tech industry.

McKinsey & Company's Leadership Development Program:

- **Overview:** McKinsey & Company, a global management consulting firm, has a Leadership Development Program that aims to prepare consultants for leadership roles within the firm and beyond.
- **Approach:** The program at McKinsey involves a combination of client work, formal training, mentorship, and peer collaboration. Consultants are exposed to a diverse range of industries and challenges, enhancing their problem-solving and leadership capabilities.
- **Results:** Graduates of McKinsey's Leadership Development Program often go on to assume leadership roles not only within McKinsey but also in client organizations, government, and the nonprofit sector. The program has been instrumental in producing leaders who contribute to shaping business strategies and solving complex organizational iss

The common thread among these programs is the integration of experiential learning, mentorship, and formal training to create a well-rounded approach to leadership development.

Jeff Immelt (Former CEO of General Electric - GE):

- **Leadership Development Program:** General Electric's Leadership Development Program (LDP).
- **Success:** Jeff Immelt is a notable graduate of GE's LDP and served as the CEO of General Electric for over a decade. His leadership at GE has been recognized for driving innovation and global expansion.

Satya Nadella (CEO of Microsoft):

- **Leadership Development Program:** While not explicitly known for a specific program, Nadella's rise through the ranks at Microsoft reflects a form of leadership development within the company.
- **Success:** Satya Nadella became the CEO of Microsoft in 2014 and has been credited with revitalizing the company's culture, emphasizing cloud computing, and fostering innovation.

James Gorman (CEO of Morgan Stanley):

- **Leadership Development Program:** Morgan Stanley's Leadership Development Program (specific details may vary).
- **Success:** James Gorman participated in leadership development initiatives at McKinsey & Company early in his career. He later became the CEO of Morgan Stanley, leading the company through strategic transformations.

Susan Wojcicki (CEO of YouTube):

- **Leadership Development Program:** Wojcicki's career trajectory involved roles at Intel and Google, where she was exposed to leadership development opportunities.
- **Success:** Susan Wojcicki, one of Google's early employees, became the CEO of YouTube and has played a significant role in the platform's growth and influence.

4. The Role of Mentorship and Coaching in Cultivating Effective Leaders

While both mentorship and coaching involve developmental relationships and the goal of fostering growth, they differ in scope, focus, structure, and the nature of the relationship. Mentorship often provides broader guidance based on personal experience, while coaching is more specific, goal-oriented, and focused on facilitating the coachee's self-discovery and performance improvement

A. Mentorship plays a pivotal role in cultivating effective leaders, offering a unique and valuable form of professional development. The importance of mentorship in leadership development extends across various dimensions:

Knowledge Transfer:

- **Experiential Learning:** Mentors, often seasoned professionals, share their wealth of experience and practical insights with mentees. This experiential learning provides mentees with a deeper understanding of real-world challenges and solutions.

Skill Development:

- **Soft Skills and Leadership Competencies:** Effective leadership extends beyond technical expertise. Mentors guide mentees in developing crucial soft skills such as communication, emotional intelligence, and interpersonal skills. They also help cultivate leadership competencies like decision-making, conflict resolution, and strategic thinking.

Career Guidance:

- **Navigating Career Paths:** Mentors offer guidance in navigating the complexities of a career, providing advice on career paths, opportunities, and potential challenges. This helps mentees make informed decisions about their professional trajectory.

Networking and Relationship Building:

- **Expanding Professional Networks:** Mentors often introduce mentees to their professional networks, creating opportunities for networking, collaboration, and exposure to diverse perspectives. Building relationships in this manner is crucial for leadership success.

Confidence Building:

- **Encouragement and Support:** Mentors serve as a source of encouragement and support, fostering mentees' self-confidence. This emotional support is essential for navigating uncertainties, taking risks, and embracing leadership roles with confidence.

Challenging Assumptions:

- **Providing Constructive Feedback:** Mentors offer constructive feedback, challenging assumptions and encouraging mentees to see situations from different angles. This helps leaders refine their perspectives and approaches.

Succession Planning:

- **Identifying and Nurturing Talent:** Organizations benefit from mentorship as a tool for identifying and nurturing future leaders. Mentors play a crucial role in succession planning by identifying and developing individuals with high leadership potential.

Cultural Integration:

- **Understanding Organizational Culture:** Mentors assist mentees in understanding and navigating organizational culture. This understanding is crucial for effective leadership, as leaders must align their actions with the values and norms of the organization.

Diversity and Inclusion:

- **Promoting Diversity:** Mentorship programs can contribute to diversity and inclusion efforts by facilitating connections between individuals from different backgrounds. This cross-cultural mentorship fosters a more inclusive leadership pipeline.

Lifelong Learning:

- **Promoting Continuous Development:** Leadership is a continuous learning journey. Mentors instill the value of lifelong learning in mentees, encouraging them to seek new skills, stay updated on industry trends, and adapt to evolving leadership challenges.

Examples: Numerous successful individuals credit their achievements, in part, to the guidance and mentorship they received. Here are examples of famous mentorships:

Warren Buffett and Benjamin Graham:

- **Mentorship:** Warren Buffett, one of the world's most successful investors, was mentored by Benjamin Graham, a renowned economist and investor. Buffett studied under Graham at Columbia Business School and adopted Graham's value investing principles, which significantly influenced Buffett's investment philosophy and success.

Oprah Winfrey and Maya Angelou:

- **Mentorship:** Oprah Winfrey, media mogul and philanthropist, considered the late Maya Angelou, a renowned poet and author, as a mentor. Angelou provided guidance and support to Oprah throughout her career, offering valuable life and career advice.

Mark Zuckerberg and Steve Jobs:

- **Mentorship:** Mark Zuckerberg, co-founder and CEO of Facebook, sought guidance from the late Steve Jobs, co-founder of Apple Inc. Jobs offered insights into building successful technology companies and navigating the challenges of leadership in the tech industry.

Bill Gates and Warren Buffett:

- **Mentorship:** Bill Gates, co-founder of Microsoft, formed a close friendship with Warren Buffett. Gates has often cited Buffett as a mentor, particularly in matters related to business strategy, philanthropy, and life choices.

Sheryl Sandberg and Larry Summers:

- **Mentorship:** Sheryl Sandberg, Chief Operating Officer of Facebook, worked closely with Larry Summers, former U.S. Treasury Secretary and Harvard University president. Summers provided mentorship to Sandberg during her time at the U.S. Treasury, influencing her career trajectory.

Elon Musk and Larry Page:

- **Mentorship:** Elon Musk, CEO of SpaceX and Tesla, has acknowledged Larry Page, co-founder of Google, as an influential mentor. Musk sought advice from Page on various business and technological challenges, highlighting the value of mentorship among tech leaders.

Maya Rudolph and Gilda Radner:

- **Mentorship:** Maya Rudolph, a successful comedian and actress, is the daughter of Minnie Riperton, a famous singer. However, she has mentioned Gilda Radner, a pioneering comedian from Saturday Night Live, as a mentor figure who inspired her comedic career.

Tim Cook and Steve Jobs:

- **Mentorship:** Tim Cook, current CEO of Apple, worked closely with Steve Jobs and considered him a mentor. Cook's operational expertise complemented Jobs' visionary leadership, and Cook played a crucial role in the success and continuity of Apple after Jobs' passing.

In summary, mentorship is a dynamic relationship that fosters the holistic development of leaders. It goes beyond the transfer of knowledge and skills, encompassing emotional support, guidance, and the cultivation of a leadership mindset. The impact of mentorship is evident in the confidence, competence, and resilience of leaders who have benefited from the wisdom and guidance of experienced mentors.

B. Coaching plays a pivotal role in cultivating effective leaders by providing personalized guidance, fostering skill development, and promoting self-awareness, enabling leaders to navigate challenges, enhance performance, and inspire their teams using these traits:

Skill Enhancement:

- **Identifying and Developing Skills:** Coaching plays a crucial role in identifying specific leadership skills that need enhancement. Coaches work with leaders to hone their communication, decision-making, emotional intelligence, and other essential skills.

Goal Setting and Alignment:

- **Defining Clear Objectives:** Coaches help leaders articulate and define their goals, aligning them with organizational objectives. This ensures that leaders are working towards outcomes that contribute to both personal and organizational success.

Performance Improvement:

- **Addressing Weaknesses and Challenges:** Effective coaching involves identifying weaknesses and challenges in a leader's performance and collaboratively developing strategies for improvement. This targeted approach contributes to overall performance enhancement.

Strategic Thinking and Decision-Making:

- **Promoting Strategic Perspectives:** Coaches guide leaders in developing strategic thinking, helping them analyze complex situations, make informed decisions, and consider long-term implications. This is crucial for navigating the complexities of leadership roles.

Enhanced Self-Awareness:

- **Facilitating Self-Reflection:** Coaching encourages leaders to reflect on their actions, behaviors, and impact. Increased self-awareness allows leaders to understand their strengths, weaknesses, and the effect of their leadership style on others.

Effective Communication:

- **Improving Communication Skills:** Coaches work with leaders to enhance their communication skills, ensuring that they can articulate a compelling vision, provide constructive feedback, and foster open dialogue within their teams.

Conflict Resolution:

- **Building Conflict Resolution Skills:** Leaders often face conflicts within their teams or organizations. Coaches assist leaders in developing effective conflict resolution strategies, fostering a positive and collaborative work environment.

Adaptability and Change Management:

- **Navigating Change:** Coaches help leaders build adaptability and resilience, essential qualities in today's dynamic business environment. Leaders learn to embrace change, navigate uncertainties, and lead their teams through transitions.

Employee Engagement and Motivation:

- **Fostering Team Dynamics:** Coaching emphasizes strategies for fostering a positive team culture, enhancing employee engagement, and motivating team members. Leaders learn to recognize and leverage the strengths of their teams.

Accountability and Goal Achievement:

- **Setting Accountability Structures:** Coaches assist leaders in establishing structures for accountability, ensuring that goals are met and that leaders take ownership of their responsibilities.

Career Development and Succession Planning:

- **Navigating Career Trajectories:** Coaches support leaders in navigating their career trajectories, providing insights into potential paths and assisting with succession planning within the organization.

Continuous Learning:

- **Promoting Lifelong Learning:** Coaching instills a mindset of continuous learning. Leaders, through coaching, recognize the importance of staying updated on industry trends, acquiring new knowledge, and adapting to evolving leadership challenges.

In summary, coaching is instrumental in cultivating effective leaders by focusing on skill development, goal alignment, performance improvement, and fostering a holistic approach to leadership. Through personalized guidance and a commitment to continuous improvement, coaching contributes significantly to the success and effectiveness of leaders in diverse organizational settings.

Examples of famous coaching relationships:

Eric Schmidt and Bill Campbell:

- **Context:** Eric Schmidt, former CEO of Google, engaged in a coaching relationship with Bill Campbell, an influential executive coach known as the "Coach of Silicon Valley."
- **Impact:** Bill Campbell's coaching played a key role in Schmidt's leadership development, particularly during Google's early years. The coaching relationship focused on strategic leadership, team dynamics, and navigating the challenges of leading a rapidly growing tech company.

Bill Gates and Marshall Goldsmith:

- **Context:** Bill Gates, co-founder of Microsoft, enlisted the services of Marshall Goldsmith, a renowned executive coach and leadership thinker.
- **Impact:** Goldsmith's coaching with Gates centered on aspects of leadership behavior, communication, and decision-making. The coaching relationship contributed to Gates' personal growth as a leader and his continued success in the technology industry.

Steve Jobs and John Wooden:

- **Context:** Steve Jobs, co-founder of Apple Inc., sought guidance from John Wooden, the legendary basketball coach, during a critical phase of Apple's development.
- **Impact:** Wooden's coaching, though not in a traditional business context, influenced Jobs' leadership style. Wooden's emphasis on character, integrity, and teamwork left a lasting impression on Jobs and contributed to the cultural values that define Apple today.

Ruth Bader Ginsburg and Kenneth Feinberg:

- **Context:** Supreme Court Justice Ruth Bader Ginsburg engaged in a coaching relationship with Kenneth Feinberg, a prominent mediator and dispute resolution expert.
- **Impact:** Feinberg's coaching focused on enhancing Justice Ginsburg's communication and negotiation skills. The coaching relationship contributed to Ginsburg's effectiveness in navigating complex legal matters and building consensus among her peers on the Supreme Court.

These examples highlight how coaching relationships, even with individuals who have reached the pinnacle of success, can contribute to ongoing growth and development in leadership. Coaches bring unique perspectives, insights, and methodologies that can have a transformative impact on leaders, regardless of their field or level of achievement.

Similarities between Mentorship and Coaching:

Developmental Relationships:

- **Mentorship:** Both mentorship and coaching involve developmental relationships aimed at fostering the growth and learning of the mentee or coachee.
- **Coaching:** In coaching, the relationship is typically focused on improving specific skills, achieving goals, or navigating challenges.

Goal Orientation:

- **Mentorship:** Mentors often help mentees set broader career or personal development goals.
- **Coaching:** Coaches work with coachees to establish specific, measurable, and achievable goals.

Feedback and Reflection:

- **Mentorship:** Both mentors and coaches provide feedback, encouraging reflection and self-awareness.
- **Coaching:** A key aspect of coaching involves providing constructive feedback and facilitating self-reflection for the coachee's continuous improvement.

Confidentiality:

- **Mentorship:** Confidentiality is often a critical aspect of mentor-mentee relationships, creating a safe space for open and honest discussions.
- **Coaching:** Coaches also adhere to confidentiality to build trust and allow coachees to share their challenges and aspirations without fear of judgment.

Differences between Mentorship and Coaching:

Scope and Focus:

- **Mentorship:** Mentors typically offer guidance on broader aspects of personal and professional development, drawing from their own experiences.
- **Coaching:** Coaching is often more specific and goal-oriented, focusing on skill enhancement, performance improvement, or addressing particular challenges.

Expertise and Experience:

- **Mentorship:** Mentors are often more experienced individuals in a similar field or industry, providing insights and advice based on their own career journey.
- **Coaching:** Coaches may or may not have direct experience in the coachee's field; their expertise lies in coaching methodologies and facilitating the coachee's learning process.

Structured vs. Informal Relationships:

- **Mentorship:** Mentor-mentee relationships may be more informal and evolve naturally, often developing over a more extended period.
- **Coaching:** Coaching relationships are often more structured, with defined timelines and specific objectives.

Role and Expectations:

- **Mentorship:** Mentors may provide guidance, share personal experiences, and offer advice based on their own journey.

- **Coaching:** Coaches focus on asking questions, active listening, and guiding the coachee to explore solutions independently, promoting self-discovery and self-direction.

Career vs. Performance Focus:

- **Mentorship:** Mentorship often has a more significant emphasis on career development, offering insights into navigating one's career trajectory.
- **Coaching:** Coaching tends to be more performance-oriented, addressing immediate challenges, improving specific skills, or achieving short-term goals.

5

Chapter 5: Training for Management

1. **Academic avenues for acquiring management skills:**

Acquiring management skills through academic avenues provides a structured and comprehensive approach to learning. Here are several academic pathways to develop management skills:

Bachelor's Degree in Business Administration (BBA):

- **Description:** A BBA program offers a foundational understanding of business principles, including management concepts, organizational behavior, and strategic planning.
- **Focus Areas:** Management, leadership, marketing, finance, human resources.

Master of Business Administration (MBA):

- **Description:** An MBA is a graduate-level program that

delves deeper into various aspects of business management, leadership, and strategy.

- **Focus Areas:** General management, specialization in areas like finance, marketing, operations, human resources.

Executive Education Programs:

- **Description:** Executive education programs are often short-term, intensive courses designed for mid-career professionals and executives to enhance their leadership and management skills.
- **Focus Areas:** Strategic management, leadership development, organizational behavior.

Leadership and Management Certificates:

- **Description:** Many universities and professional institutions offer certificates focused specifically on leadership and management, providing targeted skill development.
- **Focus Areas:** Leadership essentials, project management, change management.

Master of Management (MM) Programs:

- **Description:** Similar to an MBA, an MM program focuses on management principles but may be designed for individuals with less work experience.
- **Focus Areas:** General management, leadership, organizational strategy.

Dual Degree Programs:

- **Description:** Some universities offer dual degree programs, allowing students to combine a traditional management degree with another specialized area such as law, engineering, or public policy.
- **Focus Areas:** Varies based on the combination of degrees.

Ph.D. in Management:

- **Description:** For those interested in a research-oriented and academic career in management, a Ph.D. in Management program provides an in-depth exploration of management theories and methodologies.
- **Focus Areas:** Research methods, organizational theory, strategic management.

Professional Development Courses:

- **Description:** Various institutions and online platforms offer short-term professional development courses in specific management areas, allowing for focused and practical skill-building.
- **Focus Areas:** Time management, conflict resolution, team leadership.

Online Courses and MOOCs:

- **Description:** Massive Open Online Courses (MOOCs) provide accessible and flexible learning opportunities, often offered by top universities and institutions worldwide.
- **Focus Areas:** Leadership skills, project management, organizational dynamics.

Industry-Specific Management Programs:

- **Description:** Some industries offer specialized management programs tailored to the unique challenges and requirements of that sector.
- **Focus Areas:** Healthcare management, hospitality management, sports management.

Microcredentials and Badges:

- **Description:** Microcredentials and digital badges are gaining popularity as concise, focused programs offering specific management skills.
- **Focus Areas:** Agile management, strategic thinking, innovation.

When selecting an academic avenue, individuals should consider their career goals, level of experience, and preferred learning format (on-campus, online, part-time, full-time). Combining academic learning with practical experience through internships, projects, or work experience is essential for a well-rounded development of management skills.

1. **Professional routes to gain and improve management skills:**

Gaining and improving management skills can be achieved through various professional routes that focus on practical, hands-on experience. Here are several professional routes to gain and enhance management skills:

On-the-Job Experience:

- **Description:** Actively engaging in management responsibilities within your current role or seeking opportunities for leadership positions.
- **Benefits:** Practical application of management concepts, learning through real-world challenges, and building leadership experience.

Mentorship and Coaching:

- **Description:** Seeking mentorship from experienced managers or hiring a professional coach to provide guidance and personalized development.
- **Benefits:** Individualized support, insights from experienced leaders, and targeted skill improvement.

Leadership Training Programs:

- **Description:** Participating in leadership training programs offered by organizations, professional associations, or specialized training institutions.
- **Benefits:** Focused skill development, exposure to best practices, and networking opportunities with other aspiring leaders.

Cross-Functional Projects:

- **Description:** Taking on roles in cross-functional teams or projects that involve collaboration with different departments within an organization.

- **Benefits:** Broadening understanding of organizational dynamics, enhancing communication skills, and developing a holistic view of business operations.

Management Certifications:

- **Description:** Pursuing industry-recognized certifications in management disciplines such as project management (PMP), change management (CMC), or agile management (Scrum).
- **Benefits:** Formal recognition of expertise, validation of skills, and staying current with industry best practices.

Advanced Education:

- **Description:** Continuing education through part-time or executive programs, such as earning an MBA or enrolling in specialized management courses.
- **Benefits:** In-depth knowledge acquisition, exposure to strategic management concepts, and networking opportunities.

Professional Associations:

- **Description:** Joining relevant professional associations that offer resources, events, and networking opportunities for managers in specific industries.
- **Benefits:** Access to industry insights, continuous learning opportunities, and networking with experienced professionals.

Industry Conferences and Seminars:

- **Description:** Attending conferences, seminars, and workshops related to management and leadership in your industry.
- **Benefits:** Exposure to emerging trends, networking with industry leaders, and gaining insights from keynote speakers.

Project Leadership Roles:

- **Description:** Leading or managing projects within your organization, taking responsibility for project outcomes and team coordination.
- **Benefits:** Developing project management skills, enhancing teamwork and collaboration, and demonstrating leadership capabilities.

Online Learning Platforms:

- **Description:** Utilizing online learning platforms and Massive Open Online Courses (MOOCs) that offer management and leadership courses.
- **Benefits:** Flexible learning schedules, access to a diverse range of courses, and the ability to learn at your own pace.

Professional Networking:

- **Description:** Actively participating in professional networking events, both online and offline, to connect with other professionals in your industry.

- **Benefits:** Building a professional support network, exchanging insights, and gaining perspectives from experienced managers.

Industry-Specific Training Programs:

- **Description:** Enrolling in training programs or workshops tailored to your industry's unique management challenges and requirements.
- **Benefits:** Targeted skill development, practical knowledge application, and networking within your industry.

Combining several of these professional routes can create a well-rounded approach to gaining and improving management skills. The key is to balance theoretical knowledge with practical experience and continuously seek opportunities for growth and development.

Many individuals have successfully transitioned from technical roles to managerial positions, demonstrating the versatility and adaptability of skills. Here are a few success stories:

Satya Nadella (Microsoft):

- **Technical Background:** Satya Nadella, the current CEO of Microsoft, began his career as a technologist. He joined Microsoft as a member of the technical staff and later held various technical leadership roles, contributing to the development of cloud-based services.
- **Transition:** Nadella transitioned to managerial roles, leading Microsoft's cloud and enterprise division. His effective leadership and strategic vision played a crucial role in

Microsoft's successful transition to cloud computing. He eventually became the CEO, overseeing the company's overall operations.

Mary Barra (General Motors):

- **Technical Background:** Mary Barra started her career with General Motors (GM) as an electrical engineer. She worked in various technical roles, contributing to the development of GM vehicles.
- **Transition:** Barra successfully transitioned to managerial positions, leading global manufacturing engineering and later serving as the Vice President of Global Human Resources. She continued to climb the corporate ladder and became the CEO of General Motors, making history as the first woman to lead a major global automaker.

Sundar Pichai (Google/Alphabet):

- **Technical Background:** Sundar Pichai, the CEO of Alphabet Inc. (Google's parent company), had a technical background. He worked on the development of Google Chrome and led the Android division.
- **Transition:** Pichai transitioned to managerial roles, taking over as the CEO of Google. Under his leadership, Google experienced significant growth, and he later became the CEO of Alphabet, overseeing the broader portfolio of companies under the Alphabet umbrella.

Ursula Burns (Xerox):

- **Technical Background:** Ursula Burns started her career at Xerox as a mechanical engineering summer intern and later worked in various technical roles within the company.
- **Transition:** Burns transitioned to managerial positions, eventually becoming the CEO of Xerox. She made history as the first African American woman to lead a Fortune 500 company. Burns played a key role in steering Xerox through a transformative period, focusing on innovation and diversification.

Tim Cook (Apple):

- **Technical Background:** Tim Cook, the current CEO of Apple, started his career in the technology industry, working for companies such as IBM and Compaq.
- **Transition:** Cook transitioned to managerial roles and joined Apple as the Senior Vice President for Worldwide Operations. His operational expertise and leadership skills were crucial in streamlining Apple's supply chain and manufacturing processes. Cook eventually succeeded Steve Jobs as the CEO of Apple.

These success stories highlight how individuals with technical backgrounds can leverage their skills and expertise to excel in managerial positions, leading companies to success and innovation. Transitioning from a technical role to a managerial role often requires a combination of leadership qualities, strategic thinking, and effective communication.

In conclusion, the journey from technical expertise to managerial proficiency underscores the paramount importance of continuous learning for effective leadership. In today's dynamic business environment, ongoing learning ensures that managers remain agile, adaptable, and well-equipped to navigate evolving challenges. It is not merely a professional development strategy but a foundational element for sustained success and excellence in leadership. Embracing a mindset of continuous learning empowers managers to innovate, make informed decisions, and lead their teams with resilience in the ever-changing landscape of business and management.

6

Chapter 6: Traits and Characteristics Comparison

Key Traits and Characteristics Shared by Effective Leaders and Managers:

Communication Skills:

- **Leaders and Managers:** Effective communication is crucial for conveying vision, expectations, and providing feedback.

Decision-Making Abilities:

- **Leaders and Managers:** Both roles require sound decision-making skills to navigate challenges and drive organizational success.

Adaptability:

- **Leaders and Managers:** The ability to adapt to changing circumstances is essential for steering teams and organizations in dynamic environments.

Integrity and Ethics:

- **Leaders and Managers:** Upholding ethical standards fosters trust and credibility, whether in decision-making or daily operations.

Strategic Thinking:

- **Leaders and Managers:** Both need to think strategically, aligning actions with long-term goals and organizational vision.

Motivational Skills:

- **Leaders and Managers:** Motivating teams to achieve their best performance is a shared trait essential for driving success.

Contrasting Traits Unique to Each Role:

Leadership Traits:

- **Visionary Thinking:** Leaders often focus on inspiring and setting a compelling vision for the future.
- **Innovative Mindset:** Leaders are expected to champion innovation and guide their teams toward new ideas and

approaches.
- **Risk-Taking:** Leaders may take calculated risks to pursue opportunities for growth and change.

Management Traits:

- **Organizational Skills:** Managers excel in organizing tasks, resources, and processes to ensure efficient operations.
- **Detail-Oriented:** Managers often pay attention to specific details, ensuring tasks are executed with precision.
- **Operational Efficiency:** Managers prioritize effective implementation of strategies and plans to achieve operational goals.

Understanding and integrating these shared and unique traits is crucial for individuals in leadership and management roles. Effective leaders and managers strike a balance between these qualities, adapting their approaches based on organizational needs and the challenges at hand.

Emotional Intelligence in Leadership:

In essence, emotional intelligence is a critical aspect of both leadership and management. It empowers individuals to navigate the complexities of human interactions, build strong relationships, and foster a positive and productive work environment. Whether leading a team toward a vision (leadership) or ensuring efficient operations and team performance (management), emotional intelligence is a valuable asset.

Self-Awareness:

- **Leadership Focus:** Effective leaders possess a high level of self-awareness, understanding their own emotions, strengths, and weaknesses. This self-awareness allows them to navigate challenges with composure and authenticity.

Empathy:

- **Leadership Focus:** Empathy is a cornerstone of effective leadership. Leaders who empathize with the emotions and perspectives of their team members build strong relationships, foster trust, and create a positive work environment.

Motivation:

- **Leadership Focus:** Leaders with high emotional intelligence are often intrinsically motivated and can inspire and motivate others. Their enthusiasm and passion for the vision of the organization can drive collective efforts toward shared goals.

Social Skills:

- **Leadership Focus:** Social skills involve effective communication, conflict resolution, and relationship-building. Leaders with strong social skills can navigate complex interpersonal dynamics and create cohesive, high-performing teams.

Emotional Intelligence in Management:

Self-Regulation:

- **Management Focus:** Effective managers exhibit self-regulation, maintaining control over their emotions in challenging situations. This trait enables them to make rational decisions and manage stress effectively.

Communication:

- **Management Focus:** Managers with high emotional intelligence excel in communication. They can convey information clearly, actively listen to team members, and adapt their communication style to suit different situations.

Team Motivation:

- **Management Focus:** Motivating a team to achieve objectives is a key aspect of management. Managers with emotional intelligence can understand the needs and motivations of individual team members, tailoring their approach to inspire optimal performance.

Conflict Resolution:

- **Management Focus:** Conflict is inherent in any workplace, and managers with emotional intelligence can navigate conflicts effectively. They address issues diplomatically, seek resolutions, and maintain a positive team atmosphere.

Common Ground:

- **Collaboration:** Both leadership and management benefit from emotional intelligence when it comes to fostering collaboration. Leaders and managers who understand and manage emotions effectively can create a culture of collaboration, where individuals work together harmoniously toward shared goals.
- **Adaptability:** Emotional intelligence contributes to adaptability in both leadership and management. Leaders and managers who can understand and respond to the emotions of themselves and others can adapt their approaches to changing circumstances and challenges.

7

Chapter 7: Challenges Faced by Leaders and Managers and Strategies to Overcome Them and Foster Growth

Challenges

- Communication Breakdowns:

Challenge: Leaders and managers often face challenges in effective communication, leading to misunderstandings, decreased morale, and unproductive teams.

- Resistance to Change:

Challenge: Implementing change initiatives can be met with resistance from team members who may be comfortable with existing processes.

- Team Conflict:

Challenge: Interpersonal conflicts within teams can hinder collaboration, reduce productivity, and create a negative work environment.

  • Adapting to Change:

Challenge: Leaders and managers must navigate rapidly changing business environments, requiring them to adapt strategies and operations accordingly.

  • Employee Engagement:

Challenge: Keeping employees engaged and motivated is an ongoing challenge, particularly in the face of routine tasks or prolonged periods of uncertainty.

Strategies to Overcome Challenges and Foster Growth:

  • Effective Communication:

Strategy: Prioritize transparent and open communication. Regular team meetings, one-on-one check-ins, and the use of various communication channels can enhance understanding and build trust.

  • Change Management Strategies:

Strategy: Involve employees in the change process, communicate the reasons behind changes clearly, and provide support and training to ease the transition. Creating a culture that values innovation and continuous improvement can make change more palatable.

• Conflict Resolution Techniques:

Strategy: Implement conflict resolution training for leaders and managers. Encourage open dialogue, active listening, and mediation to address conflicts promptly. Establishing clear team norms and expectations can also prevent conflicts from escalating.

• Agile Leadership:

Strategy: Develop adaptive leadership styles. Embrace an agile mindset that allows leaders and managers to respond quickly to changing circumstances. Encourage continuous learning and provide resources for professional development.

• Employee Recognition and Development:

Strategy: Implement employee recognition programs to acknowledge and reward achievements. Offer opportunities for skill development and career advancement, demonstrating a commitment to employee growth and well-being.

• Team Building Activities:

Strategy: Organize team-building activities and exercises to foster a positive team culture. Encourage collaboration, trust-building, and a sense of camaraderie among team members.

• Strategic Goal Alignment:

Strategy: Clearly communicate organizational goals and ensure that individual and team objectives align with the overarching vision. This promotes a sense of purpose and direction, contributing to employee motivation.

• Feedback and Performance Reviews:

Strategy: Implement regular feedback sessions and performance reviews. Constructive feedback helps employees understand expectations, identify areas for improvement, and align their efforts with organizational goals.

• Employee Well-Being Initiatives:

Strategy: Prioritize employee well-being by offering wellness programs, flexible work arrangements, and mental health support. A healthy and motivated workforce is more resilient in the face of challenges.

• Crisis Management Plans:

Strategy: Develop and regularly update crisis management plans. Preparedness for unforeseen events enables leaders and managers to respond swiftly and effectively, minimizing disruption and maintaining employee confidence.

By implementing these strategies, leaders and managers can overcome challenges, nurture a positive work environment, and foster the growth and development of both individuals and the organization as a whole. The key lies in proactive leadership, effective communication, and a commitment to continuous improvement.

Examples of real-world organizations that have successfully navigated leadership and management challenges.

IBM (International Business Machines Corporation):

- **Challenge:** IBM faced significant challenges in the early 1990s, including financial struggles and a need to adapt to the changing technology landscape.
- **Solution:** Under the leadership of CEO Lou Gerstner, IBM underwent a transformative turnaround. Gerstner implemented strategic changes, focusing on services and solutions rather than just hardware. This shift revitalized the company, leading to its resurgence as a global technology and consulting leader.

Starbucks:

- **Challenge:** In the mid-2000s, Starbucks encountered challenges related to overexpansion, declining store sales, and concerns about the quality of its coffee.
- **Solution:** Howard Schultz, the founder and CEO, returned to lead Starbucks in 2008. Schultz implemented various strategies, including closing underperforming stores, refocusing on the customer experience, and introducing new products. These measures contributed to Starbucks' recovery, reaffirming its position as a leading global coffeehouse chain.

Ford Motor Company:

- **Challenge:** Ford faced financial difficulties and a changing automotive industry landscape during the 2008 global financial crisis.
- **Solution:** Alan Mulally, appointed as CEO in 2006, implemented a comprehensive restructuring plan known as the "One Ford" strategy. This involved consolidating operations, divesting non-core brands, and emphasizing innovation and sustainability. Mulally's leadership played a pivotal role in Ford's successful turnaround and resurgence in the following years.

Microsoft:

- **Challenge:** In the early 2000s, Microsoft faced challenges related to competition in the tech industry and a need to adapt to emerging trends.
- **Solution:** Satya Nadella, appointed as CEO in 2014, spearheaded a cultural transformation at Microsoft. He shifted the company's focus toward cloud computing and services, fostering collaboration and innovation. Under Nadella's leadership, Microsoft experienced a significant resurgence, becoming one of the world's most valuable technology companies.

These examples showcase how effective leadership, strategic management, and adaptive approaches can enable organizations to overcome challenges and thrive in dynamic and competitive environments. The ability to navigate change, make strategic decisions, and align organizational goals with market demands is crucial for sustained success.

Conclusion:

In conclusion, effective leadership and management are indispensable facets of organizational success. Leadership, marked by visionary thinking and inspiration, sets the direction, fostering innovation and guiding teams toward a shared vision. Management, with its focus on efficiency and operational excellence, ensures the effective execution of strategies. While leadership encourages change and creativity, management provides stability and order. The intertwining of these roles creates a powerful synergy, with leaders inspiring and managers executing. Successful coexistence involves recognizing the unique traits of each, fostering open communication, and creating a collaborative culture where the strengths of leadership and management harmonize, propelling the organization toward sustained growth and achievement.

If you found this book to be helpful and informative, I'd be very appreciative if you left a favorable review for the book on amazon. Thanks!!

Useful References:

- Bass, B. M. (1985). Leadership and Performance Beyond Expectations. Free Press.
- Covey, S. R. (1989). The 7 Habits of Highly Effective People. Free Press.

- Kotter, J. P. (1996). Leading Change. Harvard Business Review Press.
- Drucker, P. F. (1999). Management Challenges for the 21st Century. HarperBusiness.
- Goleman, D., Boyatzis, R., & McKee, A. (2002). Primal Leadership: Realizing the Power of Emotional Intelligence. Harvard Business Review Press.
- Collins, J. (2001). Good to Great: Why Some Companies Make the Leap... and Others Don't. HarperBusiness.
- Blanchard, K., & Johnson, S. (1982). The One Minute Manager. William Morrow.
- Senge, P. M. (1990). The Fifth Discipline: The Art and Practice of the Learning Organization. Doubleday.
- Maxwell, J. C. (1998). The 21 Irrefutable Laws of Leadership. Thomas Nelson.
- Carnegie, D. (1936). How to Win Friends and Influence People. Simon & Schuster.